Crazy Love Story Vol. 1

Created by Lee Vin

Translation - Sora Han
English Adaptation - Andrew Berg
Copy Editor - Peter Ahlstrom
Retouch and Lettering - Rubina Chabra
Production Artists - Anthony Daulo and James Lee
Cover Design - Anna Kernbaum

Editor - Julie Taylor
Digital Imaging Manager - Chris Buford
Pre-Press Manager - Antonio DePietro
Production Managers - Jennifer Miller and Mutsumi Miyazaki
Art Director - Matt Alford
Managing Editor - Jill Freshney
VP of Production - Ron Klamert
President and C.O.O. - John Parker
Publisher and C.E.O. - Stuart Levy

A  Manga

TOKYOPOP Inc.
5900 Wilshire Blvd. Suite 2000
Los Angeles, CA 90036

E-mail: info@TOKYOPOP.com
Come visit us online at www.TOKYOPOP.com

ISBN: 1-59182-772-8

First TOKYOPOP printing: October 2004

10 9 8 7 6 5 4 3 2 1

Printed in the USA

Crazy Love Story

Volume 1

by

Lee Vin

HAMBURG // LONDON // LOS ANGELES // TOKYO

Crazy Love Story

CONTENTS

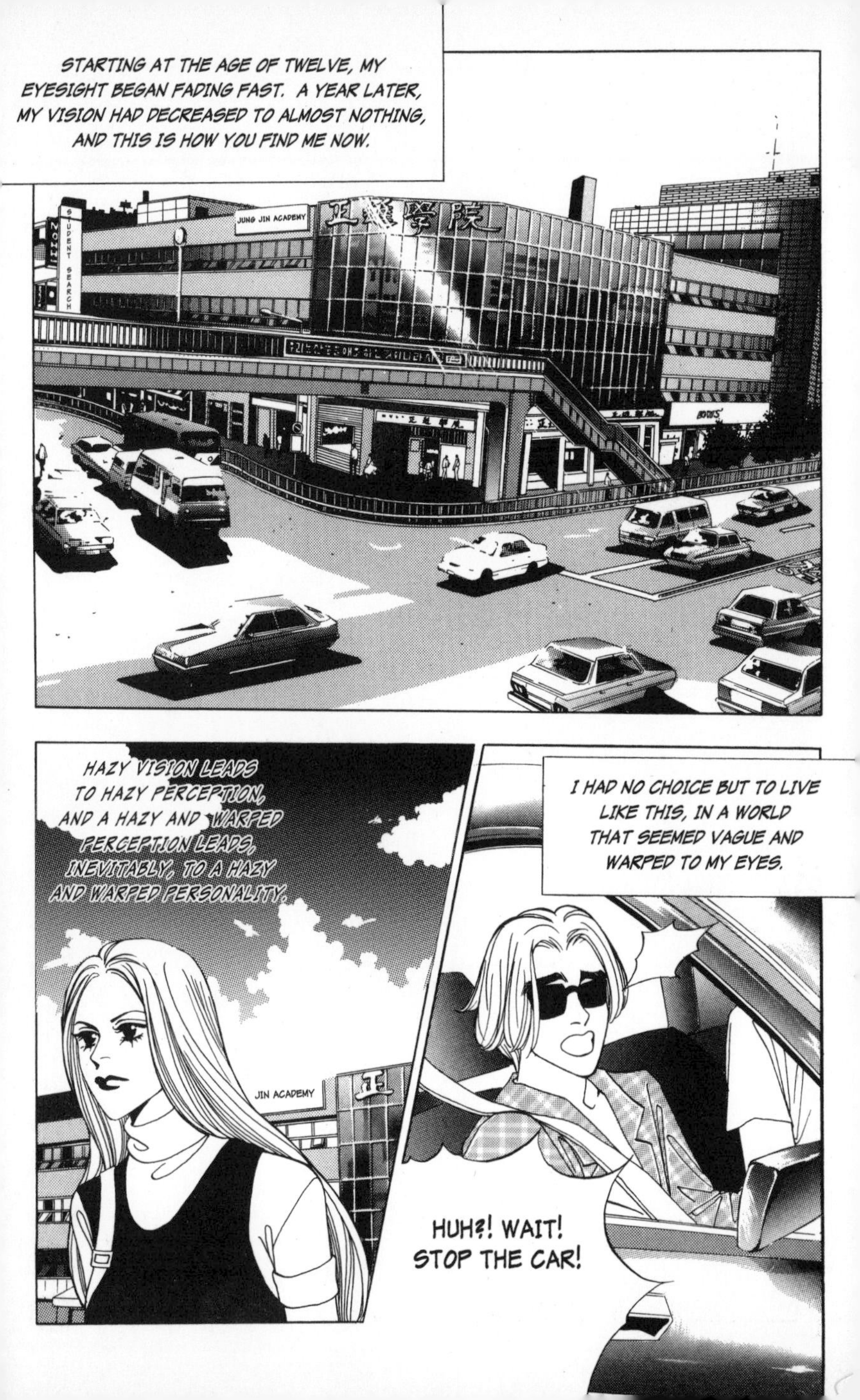

STARTING AT THE AGE OF TWELVE, MY EYESIGHT BEGAN FADING FAST. A YEAR LATER, MY VISION HAD DECREASED TO ALMOST NOTHING, AND THIS IS HOW YOU FIND ME NOW.

JUNG JIN ACADEMY

STUDENT SEARCH

HAZY VISION LEADS TO HAZY PERCEPTION, AND A HAZY AND WARPED PERCEPTION LEADS, INEVITABLY, TO A HAZY AND WARPED PERSONALITY.

JIN ACADEMY

I HAD NO CHOICE BUT TO LIVE LIKE THIS, IN A WORLD THAT SEEMED VAGUE AND WARPED TO MY EYES.

HUH?! WAIT! STOP THE CAR!

HAE JUNG!
HAE JUNG SHIN!
I'VE LIVED THAT WAY 'TIL NOW.

IT'S BEEN A LONG TIME.

IT **HAS** BEEN A LONG TIME.

WHAT... WHAT ARE YOU DOING HERE?

CAN'T YOU SEE? THE ONLY PEOPLE HERE ARE THE STUDENTS WHO FAILED THEIR COLLEGE ENTRANCE EXAMS AND ARE STUDYING TO PASS IT THE SECOND TIME AROUND.

*I DON'T WEAR GLASSES OR CONTACT LENSES. I ALMOST **ENJOY** THE HAZE AND WARP OF THIS WORLD.*

YOU FAILED THE ENTRANCE EXAM?

YOU?

IS THAT SO SURPRISING?

N-N-N-NO... I - I JUST FIGURED... THAT YOU WOULD DEFINITELY PASS...

YOU... YOU WERE ALWAYS SAYING THAT YOU WOULD MAKE IT FOR SURE.

THINGS DON'T ALWAYS TURN OUT THE WAY YOU EXPECT.

NO... I - I DIDN'T MEAN IT THAT WAY...

IT'S JUST THAT I ALWAYS THOUGHT OF YOU AS SOMEONE WHO DID EXACTLY WHAT YOU SAID YOU WOULD DO -- WHO DID WHATEVER YOU WANTED, WHATEVER YOU PUT YOUR MIND TO.

I REALLY DID BECOME A SINGER AFTER ALL. I'M DOING PRETTY WELL THESE DAYS. I'M ON TV... AND...

1995 12.7 - 12.11 KOEX
2ND Annual Seoul National Festival of Early Childhood Education
1995 12.7 - 12.11 KOEX

WON'T YOU GIVE ME ANOTHER CHANCE?

I...I STILL...

DON'T EXPECT A STRAIGHT ANSWER FROM A TWISTED PERSON.
I'M LIKE A MISCHIEVOUS FROG THAT ALWAYS SAYS THE OPPOSITE OF WHAT I MEAN.

I'VE TAPED ALL YOUR TV APPEARANCES AND WATCHED THEM A HUNDRED TIMES. I EVEN KNOW THAT IN THAT ONE INTERVIEW, YOU SAID THAT YOU'RE STILL HOOKED ON THE GIRL YOU USED TO DATE IN HIGH SCHOOL, THAT YOU CAN'T SEEM TO FORGET HER... I'VE MADE A SCRAPBOOK OF ALL THE ARTICLES WRITTEN ABOUT YOU. SO MANY TIMES I ACTUALLY WENT TO THE BROADCASTING STATIONS AND STOOD BEHIND HUNDREDS OF SCREAMING GIRLS, JUST TO CATCH A GLIMPSE OF YOU.

BUT IT'S OVER BETWEEN US. THINGS THAT HAVE ENDED ARE THROUGH FOR GOOD. THIS IS MY PERSONALITY.
I'M HAZY AND UNCLEAR...
I HAVE SO MANY REGRETS,
BUT STILL... I'M SO TWISTED.

VOL. 1
My mad princess

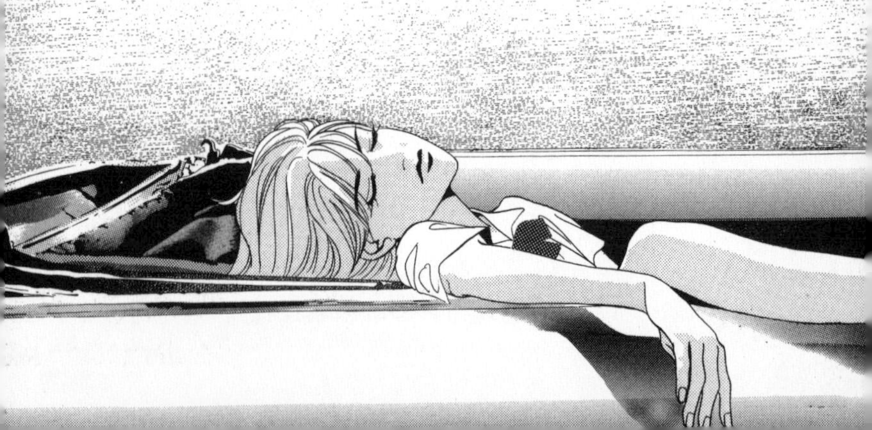

② 홍익대학교
③ 서 교 동
나가는
Way Out
HONG IK
NIVERSITY

239-03-01
함

RESTROOMS

THAT GIRL'S STILL IN HIGH SCHOOL. I BET SHE HAS HER SCHOOL UNIFORM IN THAT BAG SHE'S CARRYING.
SHUT UP!

KIDS ARE LIKE THAT NOWADAYS. IF YOU MESS WITH THEM, YOU'LL BE SORRY. YOU DON'T KNOW HOW SCARY THEY CAN BE.
0012
ToTo is a fatso...
2 Won Nang Ja. What are you doing right now? You're probably asleep. I, on the other hand, can't sleep
3 I tried to take a picture of this subway locker. I had to show all forms of ID and it was humiliating. I'm pissed off. Mister Subway Worker, one of these days I'll get my revenge.

IDIOTS! WHAT D'YA MEAN, SCARY? YOU'LL TALK BEHIND MY BACK, BUT YOU WON'T SAY IT TO MY FACE.

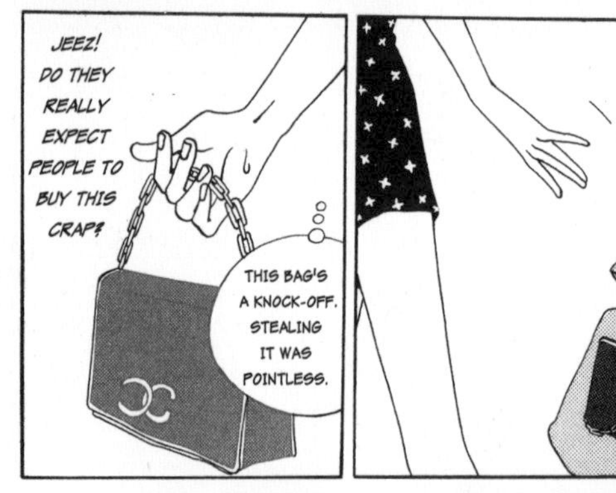

JEEZ! DO THEY REALLY EXPECT PEOPLE TO BUY THIS CRAP?
THIS BAG'S A KNOCK-OFF. STEALING IT WAS POINTLESS.

HEY! CHECK IT OUT! IT'S BRAND NEW... LET'S TAKE IT!
HURRY, BOSS! SOMEONE'S COMING.
THE LOOK-OUTS, DO HEE AND TOTO.

THREE BEGGARS LIVING NEAR H UNIVERSIT

NICE!

WHAT D'YA MEAN, "NICE"? THAT WAS OUR BALL. HOW CAN IT BE NICE WHEN YOU KNOCKED IN SOMEONE ELSE'S BALL?!

IF I PUT IT IN, THEN IT'S MY BALL. SCREW THE RULES.

WHOEVER KNOCKS IN THE MOST BALLS WINS -- THAT'S THE ONLY RULE FROM NOW ON.
GOT A PROBLEM WITH THAT?
WHAT...
I DO WHAT I WANT IF PEOPLE GO ALONG WITH IT, THAT'S THEIR PROBLEM.
딱
I KNOW THEY'RE JUST TAGGING ALONG BECAUSE THEY LOOK UP TO ME.

WHERE SHOULD WE GO NEXT?

HEY! WHO DOES SHE THINK SHE IS?
TAKE IT EASY! SHE'S THE ONE PAYING OUR WAY.

DANCE CLUB
MOSCH
Napoleone
RIKIRIKI
MONTE NAPOL E
ROCK DANCE CLUB

DAMN! THE PICKINGS ARE PRETTY SLIM TODAY.
THE NIGHT'S STILL YOUNG...

...THOSE GUYS OVER THERE LOOK OKAY.
GNR
WHAT? THOSE GUYS ARE IN HIGH SCHOOL. JUST LOOK AT THEM, THEY'RE TOTAL DORKS.

EXCUSE ME, BUT... IF YOU GIRLS ARE ALONE... MAYBE YOU'D LIKE TO JOIN US.

CAN'T YOU SEE YOU'RE BUGGING US? WHY DON'T YOU GO BACK WHERE YOU CAME FROM...
I FIND IT BENEATH ME TO ANSWER PICK-UP LINES. I ALWAYS LET SOMEONE ELSE DO IT.

IF YOU'RE HERE ALONE, YOU MUST BE LOOKING FOR A DATE.

OF COURSE THAT'S WHY WE'RE HERE. BUT WE'RE NOT INTERESTED IN HIGH SCHOOL KIDS.

FORCE DEUX
YOU LOOK LIKE YOU'RE IN HIGH SCHOOL, TOO... IN FACT...
GN

...I THINK I'VE SEEN HER AT SCHOOL BEFORE.

FORCE DEUX
AT SCHOOL? WAS THERE A GUY LIKE THAT AT SCHOOL?
I KEEP MY SCHOOL LIFE COMPLETELY SEPARATE FROM MY NIGHTLIFE, S NO ONE SHOUL RECOGNIZE M HERE.
THAT'S A LIE.
I'M SERIOUS. I EVEN KNOW YOUR NAME. HAE JUNG SHIN.

YOU'RE ON THE HONORS LIST.

EVERYONE AT SCHOOL KNOWS YOU.

THAT WAS HOW WE MET.

YEAH, RIGHT! HER? ALL SHE DOES IS PARTY! HONORS STUDENT?!
THAT'S RIDICULOUS.

OKAY. FINE. WE'LL PARTY WITH YOU GUYS. COME JOIN US AT OUR TABLE.

WHY? ARE YOU SCARED I'LL SPREAD RUMORS ABOUT YOU?

HARDLY! I DON'T CARE IF YOU SPREAD RUMORS OR NOT.
weiser
와이저

HOW DID YOU RECOGNIZE ME IN A PLACE LIKE THIS?
BECAUSE I'M INTERESTED IN YOU!
BUT I DON'T RECOGNIZE YOU AT ALL.
OF COURSE NOT. I'M NOT A TOP STUDENT LIKE YOU. I'M JUST AN AVERAGE STUDENT-- PRETTY ORDINARY, REALLY.
C'MON! LET'S GO OUT AND PARTY!
OK!
YOU CAN'T BE THAT ORDINARY. I MEAN, YOU'RE HERE, AREN'T YOU?
UNLESS THERE'RE NO ORDINARY STUDENTS LEFT IN THE WORLD...
FORCE DEUX FORCE
I DON'T DO MUCH ELSE. I JUST COME HERE TO DANCE. I LOVE TO DANCE, THAT'S WHY.

HEY! NOW I REMEMBER-- IT'S HIM!
THE GUY WHO NEVER GOES TO CLASS.
I HEARD HE'S A DJ IN ITAEWON--AND ALSO HERE IN SEOUL--AND THAT HE HOOKED HIMSELF UP WITH AN AGENT. RUMOR HAS IT HE'S GOING TO BE A POP STAR PRETTY SOON. I GUESS THAT'S WHY HE NEVER SHOWS UP AT SCHOOL.
WHAT A BLEACHED BLOND FREAK! I THINK THE HYDROGEN PEROXIDE WENT TO HIS BRAIN.

DOES THAT LOOK ON YOUR FACE MEAN YOU RECOGNIZE ME, TOO?

THAT'S RIGHT. HEY, LET'S GET OUTTA HERE!
I'M SICK OF THIS PLACE.

THEY'RE LEAVING TOGETHER.
I GUESS THEY DECIDED TO HOOK UP. NOW THE REST OF US HAVE TO PICK PARTNERS.
ARRGH! I WANTED THAT GIRL!
NIRVANA

LOOK, THERE'S A CAR! IF YOU WANT TO HANG OUT WITH ME, THERE'S ONE CONDITION.

FROM NOW ON, WHATEVER IT TAKES, YOU HAVE TO AMUSE ME!

VOL. 2
She is
"mad in heaven"

I'M LYING FACE UP IN THE MIDDLE OF THE FREEWAY...

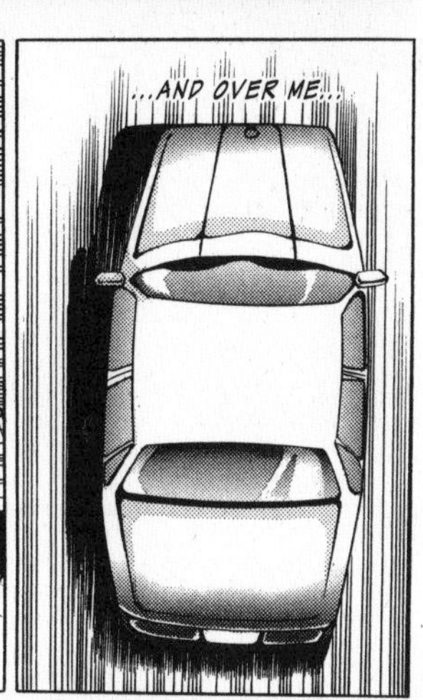

EVERY NIGHT...
I'M HAUNTED BY
THIS SAME
RECURRING
DREAM.

THE FIRST THING YOU HAVE TO DO IS...
I BEGAN HAVING THIS DREAM AROUND THE SAME TIME MY EYESIGHT WENT BAD... MAYBE THE DREAM WAS STEALING MY VISION.

BALANCE
coffee & beverage 322-6197
...STEAL THAT CAR!

H-HOW?! WE DON'T HAVE THE KEYS.

THAT'S WHY YOU HAVE TO STEAL IT! STUPID!

HAVEN'T YOU EVER WATCHED MACGYVER? USE A WIRE OR A HAIRPIN TO PICK THE LOCK. DO WHATEVER IT TAKES.
S-STILL... YOU DON'T HAVE TO CALL ME STUPID...

I DON'T HAVE A WIRE OR A HAIRPIN.
FORCE DE
WAIT.

HERE!

!

Y-YOU LOOK MUCH PRETTIER WITH YOUR HAIR DOWN!
VERY FUNNY. NOW SHUT UP AND PICK THE LOCK!

THE PIN'S TOO BIG FOR THE KEYHOLE.
WAIT.

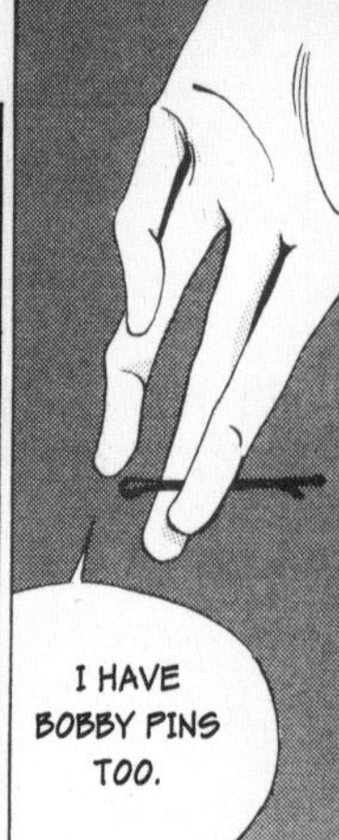
I HAVE BOBBY PINS TOO.

I-I'VE NEVER DONE THIS BEFORE. IT'S NOT WORKING...
HEY, YOU! WHAT ARE YOU DOING TO MY CAR?!

WHAT THE HELL ARE YOU...

N-NOW WHAT? I DIDN'T MEAN TO! IT WAS JUST A REFLEX!

NICE JOB.

HERE ARE THE KEYS!

AH HA HA HA HA!
6 광화문 시청
연세대

WHAT DO YOU THINK? ISN'T THIS FUN? YOU'VE NEVER DONE ANYTHING LIKE THIS BEFORE, HAVE YOU?
ME? UH-UH...
서울 1
추1558

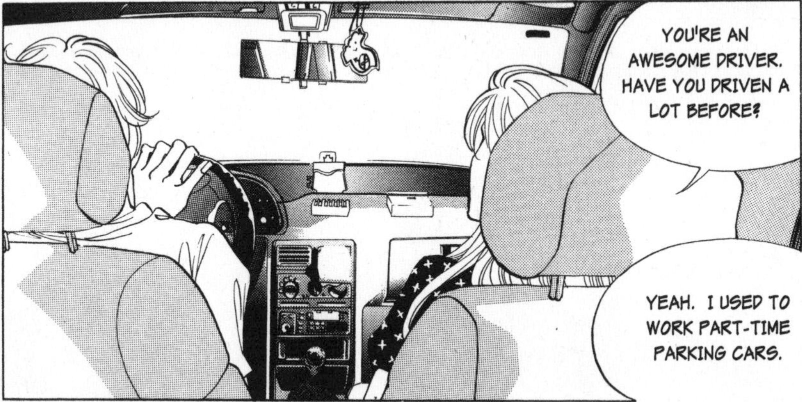
YOU'RE AN AWESOME DRIVER. HAVE YOU DRIVEN A LOT BEFORE?
YEAH. I USED TO WORK PART-TIME PARKING CARS.

IN NINTH GRADE, WHILE WE WERE ALL TAKING OUR HIGH SCHOOL ENTRANCE EXAMS, MY MOTHER PASSED AWAY.

ME AND THE GUYS I WORKED WITH USED TO TAKE THE CUSTOMERS' CARS OUT AND DRIVE AROUND.

AFTER SHE SPOKE TO THE TEACHER...

I WAS IN THE MIDDLE OF THE TEST WHEN MY AUNT CAME TO GET ME.

YOUR MOTHER'S JUST PASSED AWAY. YOU BETTER HURRY UP AND GO HOME.

IS THERE A STUDENT BY THE NAME OF HAE JUNG SHIN HERE?

I'M NOT GOING ANYWHERE.

CHECK HER OUT!
WHAT THE HELL?
WHAT?

ARE YOU SAYING I SHOULD FAIL MY TEST AND NOT GO TO HIGH SCHOOL?

SO, I GOT A PERFECT SCORE ON MY HIGH SCHOOL ENTRANCE EXAM, GRADUATED JUNIOR HIGH WITH HONORS AND ENTERED HIGH SCHOOL WITH HONORS.

MY MOM HAD BEEN SICK FOR A LONG TIME.

TAKING CARE OF HER WAS EXHAUSTING FOR THE WHOLE FAMILY.

HER DEATH WAS A GOOD THING. FOR EVERYONE.

IT HAPPENED LATE ONE NIGHT AS I WAS HEADING HOME FROM THE LIBRARY. I HAD JUST STARTED HIGH SCHOOL.

GET HOME SAFELY!
BYE!

SOMEONE WAS FOLLOWING ME.

I TURNED AROUND.

IT WAS MY MOM!

I WAS TERRIFIED. WHETHER IT WAS MY MOM... OR SOMEONE ELSE... I'D JUST SEEN A GHOST.

I RAN.

STOP FOLLOWING ME! PLEASE GO AWAY! MOM! I HAD NO CHOICE! YOU ALWAYS TOLD ME NOT TO GET ATTACHED, NOT TO GET EMOTIONAL THAT I SHOULDN'T EVEN CRY IF YOU DIED.

I CAN'T HELP IT
IF I WAS BORN
TWISTED AND COLD-HEARTED!

IT'S JUST THE WAY I AM.

OPEN THE DOOR!

OPEN THE DOOR!

WHAT'S WRONG, HAE JUNG?!

SISTER, EEEK! SISTER!

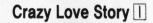

AFTER THAT NIGHT, MY MOM KEPT FOLLOWING ME. ALL THE GROWN-UPS TOLD ME IT WAS MOM'S WAY OF HELPING ME LET GO OF HER. SHIT! I HAD NOTHING TO LET GO OF IN THE FIRST PLACE.

WHAT'S WRONG? ARE YOU OKAY?

STOP THE CAR!

WHAT'S WRONG?! WHAT ABOUT THE CAR?

LEAVE IT!

JUST LEAVE IT ANYWHERE!
WE WERE GOING TO DITCH IT ANYWAY!

EH?
HMPH!

WAIT!

W-WAIT! IT'S DIRTY.

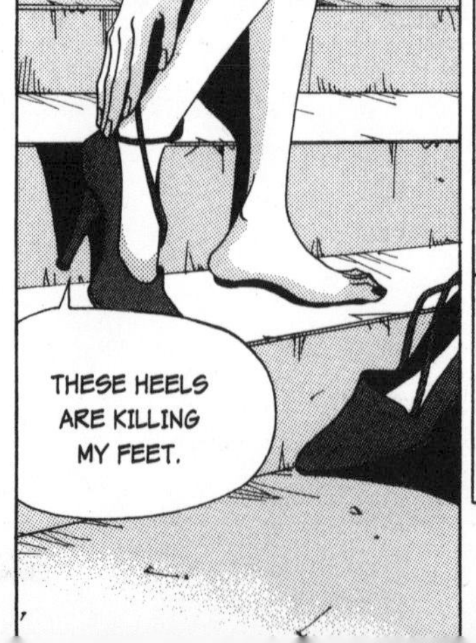
THESE HEELS ARE KILLING MY FEET.

SIT ON THIS.

FORCE DEUX

LOOK AT YOU! TRYING TO BE A GENTLEMAN!

YOU REALLY SHOULDN'T SMOKE.

WHAT?
IT DOESN'T SUIT YOU.

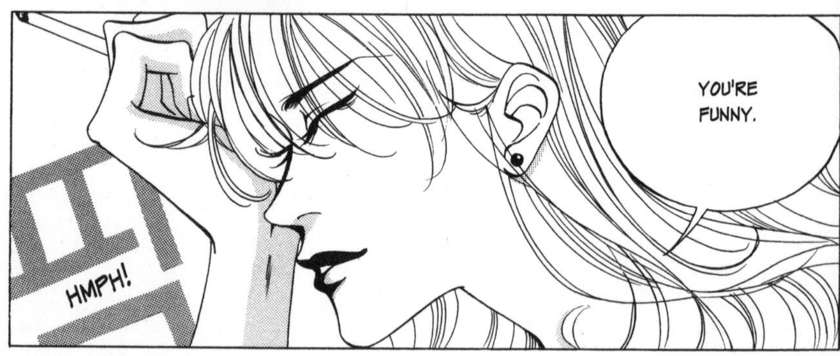
YOU'RE FUNNY.
HMPH!

LET'S GET ONE THING STRAIGHT!
THERE'S NOTHING I HATE MORE THAN PEOPLE TELLING ME WHAT TO DO AND WHAT NOT TO DO.

I'M JUST TELLING YOU WHAT I THINK.

YOU'RE PURE AND BEAUTIFUL. SOMETHING THAT CRUDE DOESN'T SUIT YOU.

ON TOP OF THAT, YOU DON'T NEED ALL THAT MAKEUP, EITHER. YOU'RE PERFECT JUST THE WAY YOU ARE.

THAT'S THE TRUTH MY BEAUTIFUL, CRAZY PRINCESS

YOUR ESSENCE IS BEAUTIFUL AS IT IS. IT'S... SO RARE TO FIND SOMEONE WHOSE ESSENCE IS BEAUTIFUL. IT'S SOMETHING PRECIOUS.

YOU WERE ALWAYS RADIANT AND BEAUTIFUL, AN ICE PRINCESS WHO GREW TWISTED AND CRUEL WITH ICICLES EMBEDDED IN HER HEART-- LIVING IN HER ICE CASTLE, DISCOURAGING ANYONE FROM APPROACHING, ANYONE FROM COMING CLOSER

YOU'RE... YOU'RE SO CLOSE... I CAN'T BELIEVE IT...

UM... UH...
WHAT IS IT?
I HEARD THAT...
...WHEN GIRLS... HAVE THEIR PERIOD... THEY GET AN URGE TO STEAL THINGS. ARE... ARE YOU LIKE THAT TOO?

IDIOT! WHERE DID YOU HEAR SUCH A STUPID THING?

IT'S NOT LIKE THAT?
NO, IT'S NOT!

TH-THEN... FROM NOW ON, IF YOU WANT SOMETHING, JUST TELL ME.
AND YOU'LL STEAL IT FOR ME?

NO! WHATEVER IT IS, I'LL BUY IT FOR YOU!

DO YOU HAVE A LOT OF MONEY?
NO, I DON'T HAVE MUCH.

THEN HOW ARE YOU GOING TO BUY IT FOR ME?
I'LL MAKE MONEY AND BUY IT FOR YOU.

I'LL GET A PART-TIME JOB!
IS THIS GUY NAÏVE? OR JUST PLAIN STUPID? FROM WHAT I'VE HEARD, HE'S A BIT OF A BAD BOY.

AND HOW CAN I PAY YOU BACK...
...FOR SAYING YOU'LL BUY ME ANYTHING I WANT?

Come on!
HUH?

HER KISS WAS A KISS MADE IN HEAVEN!
SHE'S MY CRAZY ANGEL...
SHE'S MY CRAZY PRINCESS...
THAT'S IT! I'VE MADE A DECISION. FROM NOW ON, I'M GOING TO LOVE YOU.
YOU'RE MY CRAZY ANGEL...
YOU'RE MY CRAZY PRINCESS...
YOU'RE MY CRAZY LOVE.

2 - 1

HEY! HAE JUNG SHIN!
I TOLD YOU NOT TO MISS THE MORNING REVIEW SESSION! WHAT ARE YOU GONNA DO NOW? YOU MISSED IT AGAIN!
RELAX! EVEN WITHOUT IT, I GET BETTER GRADES THAN YOU.

HELLO!

WHAT ARE YOU DOING HERE?

I'VE DECIDED TO COME TO SCHOOL EVERY DAY FROM NOW ON.

THAT'S NOT WHAT I MEANT. YOU WERE NEVER IN MY CLASS BEFORE!

FROM NOW ON, I'M IN YOUR CLASS.

AH... I HEARD THAT SOMEONE TRANSFERRED FROM THE LITERATURE DEPARTMENT TO OUR FIELD.
THIS FIELD IS VERY DIFFERENT FROM LINGUISTICS, AND THE WORK IS VERY DIFFICULT, SO I HOPE YOU'LL TRY YOUR BEST.
SUNG MOO JIN, PLEASE COME TO THE FRONT AND INTRODUCE YOURSELF TO YOUR CLASSMATES.
2 - 1
(HE'S NOT A VERY GOOD STUDENT! WHY DID HE HAVE TO TRANSFER TO THIS DEPARTMENT...? OUR CLASS AVERAGE IS GOING TO GO DOWN. SHIT!)
YES, SIR.
HELLO, STUDENTS OF GRADE TWO, CLASS ONE. I'M SUNG MOO JIN. I'M VERY PLEASED TO MEET YOU ALL.
THAT'S IT?
THAT'S THE GUY WHO'S KNOWN FOR BEING A GOOD DANCER!

HEY! SING A SONG, OR DANCE A LITTLE BEFORE YOU GO BACK TO YOUR SEAT!
THAT'S RIGHT! DANCE!
SHOULD I?
YES, YES!
DO IT!
HYUP!
KYAH!
HOO-HOO!
WOW! HE'S SO COOL!

YOUR KISS IS MADE IN HEAVEN.
YOU'RE MY CRAZY ANGEL.
YOU'RE MY CRAZY PRINCESS.
YOU'RE MY CRAZY LOVE.
I'VE MADE UP MY MIND.
FROM NOW ON,
I'M GOING TO LOVE YOU.

VOL. 3
Her boyfriend, Jimmy

WHO DID YOU COME LOOKIN' FOR? LADY IN THE CAFÉ THIS LATE AT NIGHT...
YELLOW STRANDS AND RED LIPSTICK...
YOU'RE FEELI THE LOVE... AN CASTING A SMI AT ME, INCHIN CLOSER TO YO
SORROW SWIRLING AROUND YOUR SLENDER SHOULDERS... LIKE WISPS OF SMOKE...
BUT THE WORD... THAT YOU CAN'T GIVE YOUR HEART AWAY...
TOUCHING OUR WINE GLASSES TOGETHER... CHAN CHAN CHAN!
THE ATMOSPHERE HAS OVERWHELMED HIM.

...THOSE WORDS... THAT YOU CANNOT LOVE...
HUH? HEY! WHY'D YOU STOP?
WHAT ARE YOU DOING?

SHE'S NOT
EVEN PAYING
ATTENTION...
I'VE BEEN DANCING
LIKE A FOOL THIS
ENTIRE TIME JUST
TO IMPRESS YOU
SO YOU'D THINK
I'M SUAVE...
HUH?
WHAT'S WRONG
WITH HIM?

SHE WASN'T WATCHING ME...

WHAT ARE YOU LOOKING AT?

HEY, HEY! THAT'S ENOUGH NOW! PREPARE FOR YOUR FIRST CLASS! THAT'S THE END OF OUR MORNING MEETING!
AHEM.

ATTENTION! SALUTE!
THANK YOU!

I'M... BO NA...

I'M BO NA LIM.
I HOPE WE'LL BECOME GOOD FRIENDS.

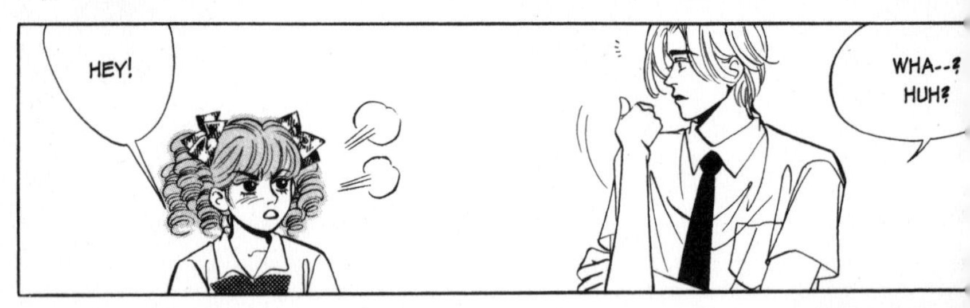

HEY!
WHA--? HUH?

THAT'S SO RUDE. I WAS INTRODUCING MYSELF, AND YOU WEREN'T EVEN LISTENING.

MY NAME IS BO NA LIM, AND I SIT RIGHT NEXT TO YOU.

OH, REALLY...

WHY DID YOU TRANSFER TO THIS DEPARTMENT ALL OF A SUDDEN? DO YOU GET GOOD GRADES?

OR MAYBE YOUR FUTURE GOALS HAVE CHANGED?

EY!
I KNOW! I WAS LISTENING.

WHY DID YOU CHANGE TO THIS DEPARTMENT? ARE YOU A GOOD STUDENT?
NOPE, I'M A LOUSY STUDENT.

OW! YOU'RE JUST LIKE ME. I'M NOT A VERY OOD STUDENT EITHER! LET'S SHAKE HANDS! SHAKE!

I'M NOT VERY STUDIOUS YSELF, BUT THIS GUY I LIKE NAMED JUN WON KANG GOES TO J UNIVERSITY AND IS IN THE PHYSICS DEPARTMENT THERE.
SO, IN ORDER TO GET INTO THE SAME DEPARTMENT AS HIM, I HAD NO CHOICE BUT TO TRANSFER TO THIS DEPARTMENT, TOO.

JUN WON KANG? YOU MEAN THAT GUY WHO LOOKS LIKE AN AIRHEAD FROM THE MUSICAL GROUP "SAINT"?
OH MY! WELL! STILL, JUN WON IS A SCHOLAR! HE GETS GOOD GRADES, EVEN THOUGH HE'S BUSY WITH HIS SINGING CAREER AND HIS SCHOOLWORK.

WHAT A JERK!
THIS GIRL IS SO LOUD... AND WHAT'S UP WITH THE GIRLY HAIRSTYLE?

HEY! DON'T TALK BADLY ABOUT JUN WON!
OR I'LL NEVER FORGIVE YOU!

BOTH OF YOU AR TOTAL AIRHEADS I'M SURE YOU'LL MAKE A GOOD COUPLE.

THANKS, THANKS!
DID NOT HEAR THE FIRST PART OF THE SENTENCE. ONLY HEARD "YOU'LL MAKE A GOOD COUPLE." SHE ONLY HEARS WHAT SHE WANTS TO.
I'LL BUY YOU A COFFEE! C'MON!

HOW COME YOU TRANSFERRED INTO OUR CLASS? HUH?
HOT & COLD DRINKS

BECAUSE OF HAE JUNG SHIN.

HAE JUNG? WHY?
BECAUSE I LIKE HAE JUNG.
YOU LIKE HAE JUNG?
OH MY! OH MY! THAT'S TOO BAD! WHAT ARE YOU GONNA DO?!
HAE JUNG HAS A BOYFRIEND!

HE DOESN'T GO TO OUR SCHOOL. YOU KNOW YANNO, THE INTERNATIONAL SCHOOL ONE SUBWAY STOP FROM HERE? HE GOES THERE. HE WAS BORN AND RAISED IN HONG KONG, BUT HE MOVED HERE. HE'S TOTALLY A WEIRDO.

HE'S REALLY SHORT AND WEARS HIGH HEELS LIKE GIRLS WEAR. HE'S GOT SKY BLUE HAIR AND YELLOW CONTACT LENSES...

HE'S GOT A REALLY BAD TEMPER, TOO. I HEARD THAT IF HAE JUN GOES OUT WITH OTHER GUY HE TAKES OFF HIS BELT AN BEATS HER WITH IT. MAYBE HE'S A PERVERT OR SOMETHING.

HAE JUNG HAS A PRETTY BAD TEMPER HERSELF, BUT SHE'S NOTHING COMPARED TO HIM.

HOW DO YOU KNOW? HOW DO YOU KNOW ALL THESE THINGS ABOUT HAE JUNG?
ME? I'M HAE JUNG'S FRIEND.

HER BEST FRIEND!
CRUMPLE

SHIT! I DON'T KNOW WHAT'S WHAT...

EVERYTHING'S SO CONFUSING. I CAN'T TELL ONE THING FROM THE NEXT.

EVERYONE SEEMS PSYCHOTIC. MAYBE THEY'RE ALL NUTS.

THERE'S HAE JUNG, THE BEST STUDENT IN THE WHOLE SCHOOL, WHO PUTS ON MAKEUP, CHANGES CLOTHES AND GOES OUT TO PARTY AND PICK UP GUYS AT ROCK CAFÉS AFTER SCHOOL.

THEN, THERE'S HAE JUNG'S CONTROLLING BOYFRIEND WHO SOMETIMES BEATS HER WITH HIS BELT.

THEN, THERE'S THE MOST PSYCHOTIC ONE OF ALL. THAT GIRL. BO NA.

BY LIKING HAE JUNG...

...I FEEL LIKE I'VE SUDDENLY ENTERED A STRANGE NEW WORLD.

THAT'S RIGHT. THIS IS A STRANGE WORLD. A WORLD TOTALLY DIFFERENT FROM THE ONE I'VE LIVED IN 'TIL NOW...

I JUST LIKE TO GO OUT AND DANCE. MY HAIR IS BLEACHED WITH HYDROGEN PEROXIDE (BECAUSE MY MOM WON'T GIVE ME MONEY TO DYE IT AT THE HAIR SALON).

I WEAR MY JEANS RIPPED, AND I GREW OUT MY BANGS TO BE MORE STYLISH. I'M JUST A GUY WHO LIKES TO PARTY.

USUALLY, I NEVER TALK MUCH IN CLASS

AT LEAST, THAT'S HOW I WAS UNTIL I MET HAE JUNG.
HUH?

HERE ARE YOU OING? AREN'T OU GOING TO STUDY HALL?

I HAVE A PRIVATE TUTOR, SO I DON'T GO TO STUDY HALL.

HA! LIAR! YOU'RE GONNA GO OUT AND PARTY RIGHT NOW.

WHAT BUSINESS IS THAT OF YOURS, ANYWAY?

HUH?

ARE YOU THE SAME HAE JUNG... THE ONE WHO WAS SO NICE TO ME? THE ONE WHO LOOKED AT ME AND SMILED... THE ONE WHO KISSED ME?
HAE JUNG! WAIT!
WHY ARE YOU BEING SO COLD? WHY ARE YOU ACTING LIKE YOU DON'T KNOW ME?

I WAS SO HAPPY BECAUSE... I'VE HAD A CRUSH ON YOU FOR SO LONG, AND YOU FINALLY SHOWED SOME INTEREST.
HAE JUNG!
WHAT YOU'RE ANNOYI

WHAT IS IT? DO YOU HAVE SOMETHING TO SAY?
N-NO... UM...
IF YOU NOTHIN SAY.

GO...
...AWAY!

HOW ANNOYING!

I'M NOT CRYING BECAUSE I HURT MY BODY, OR MY PRIDE, BY GETTING KICKED DOWN THE STAIRS BY A GIRL.

IT'S BECAUSE I THOUGHT HAE JUNG WAS INTERESTED IN ME, BECAUSE I THOUGHT SHE LIKED ME, BUT NOW... I FEEL LIKE I WAS WRONG.

IT'S BECAUSE SHE CALLED ME ANNOYING.

BUT I'M NOT GOING TO LET THAT STOP ME.

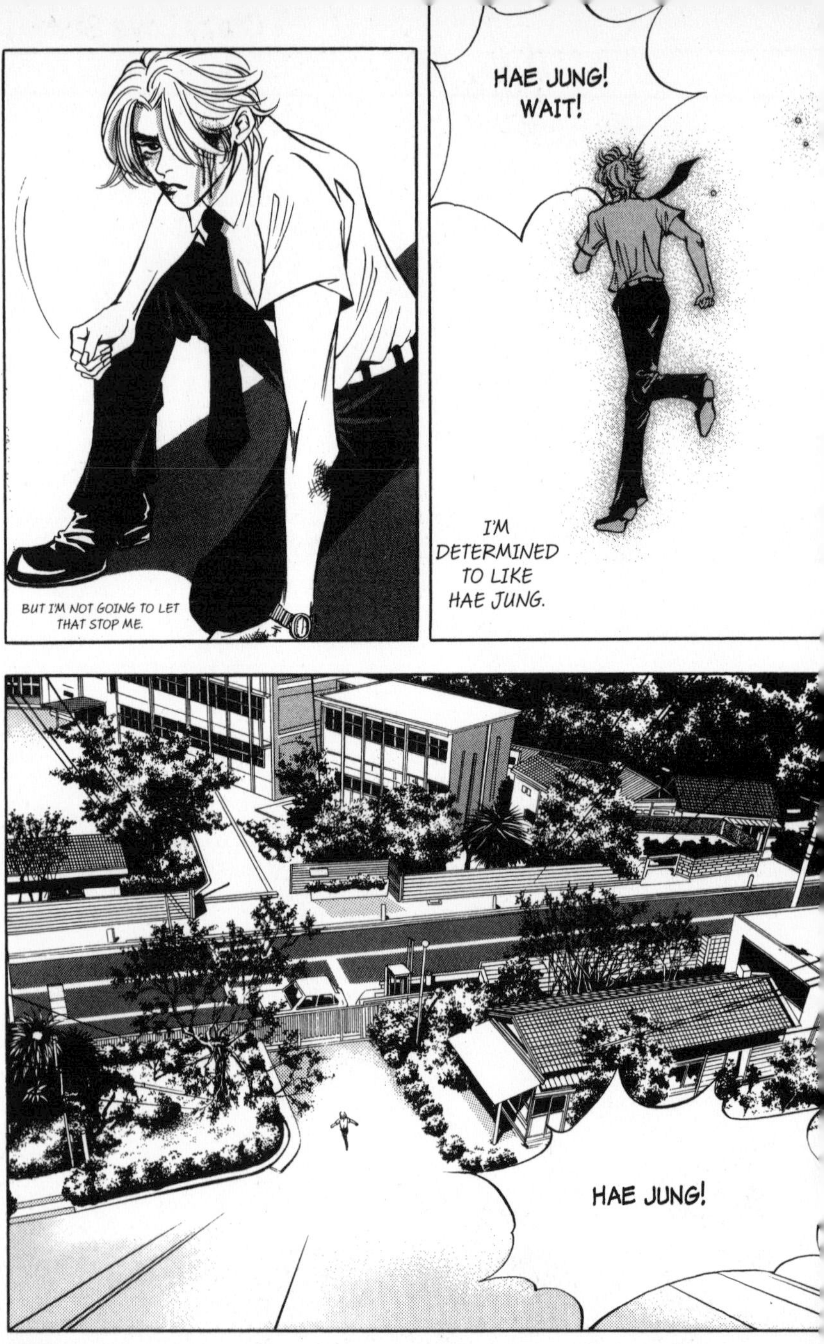

HAE JUNG! WAIT!
I'M DETERMINED TO LIKE HAE JUNG.

HAE JUNG!

IT'S HIM!
HER BOYFRIEND!
Kawasaki

WHO THE HELL IS HE? I GUESS YOU'VE MADE ANOTHER CRAZY FOOL FALL HEAD OVER HEELS IN LOVE WITH YOU.

GET OFF!

NTIL YOU'VE REPENTED, DON'T EVEN THINK OF SEEING ME!

WHO IS THAT GUY?

JIMMY.

JIMMY...

THANKS TO YOU, I WON'T BE ABLE TO SEE JIMMY FOR A WHILE.

SNIFF SNIFF...

THIS WASN'T THE SAME HAE JUNG WHO WAS ALWAYS CONFIDENT, COMMANDING AND POWERFUL.

MAYBE EVERYONE REALLY HAS GONE CRAZY. WHAT IS UP WITH THESE PEOPLE? THEY AREN'T NORMAL.

SNIFF SNIFF SOB....

AND WHAT'S UP WITH THAT JIMMY CHARACTER? IS HE FILMING A MOVIE? IS HE SOME KIND OF HONG KONG MOVIE STAR? ARE THOSE WORDS COMING OUT OF HIS MOUTH SOME KIND OF FILM SCRIPT DIALOGUE? DOES HE ALWAYS TALK LIKE THAT?

WHAT'S UP WITH THE WEIRD HAIR COLOR? WHAT'S THE DEAL WITH THOSE YELLOW EYES?

WHAT'S WITH THE SUPER-LOUD MOTORCYCLE AND HIGH-HEELED BOOTS? MAYBE HE'S SOME KIND OF HARDCORE NEO-NAZI.

WHAT'S HIS DEAL? I DON'T THINK HE'S A TRENDY PSYCHO. I THINK HE'S JUST PLAIN NUTS.

SNIFF...

WHERE ARE YOU GOING? ARE YOU GONNA FOLLOW THAT GUY?

JIMMY SAID HE'S NOT GOING OUT WITH ME TONIGHT, SO I MIGHT AS WELL GO TO THE LIBRARY AND STUDY.

SOB SOB...
I WAS SO CONFUSED. CLEARLY THOSE TWO WERE CRAZY AND WERE LIVING IN THEIR OWN INSANE LITTLE WORLD.

I'D WANDERED INTO THAT STRANGE WORLD, TOO.

OH MY!
WHAT'LL WE DO?
YOU'RE HURT PRETTY BAD!
WHERE DID YOU COME FROM?
I SAW THE WHOLE THING.
BEND DOWN A LITTLE! I CAN'T REACH. YOU'RE TOO TALL!
I SAW HAE JUNG KICK YOU DOWN THE STAIRS.
HAE JUNG IS AWESOME.
SHE KICKED YOU RIGHT OVER, EVEN THOUGH YOU'RE SO TALL!

BO NA HAS EVERY CONCEIVABLE THING IN HER BAG. FIRST AID KIT, KEY RINGS, COOKIES, CHOCOLATES, BOTTLED WATER, ETC.

MOTOR

VOL. 4
No risk, No gain!

YOU SHOULD TAKE SOME MEDICINE. WHAT IF YOUR CONDITION GETS WORSE LATER?
IT'S ALL RIGHT. THANKS FOR EVEN THIS MUCH.

EAT THIS!
I WONDER WHAT ELSE SHE HAS IN THAT BAG.

WANT TO COME WITH ME?

WHERE ARE YOU GOING?
YOU SHOULD DRINK SOME WATER, TOO.

TO WHERE JIMMY AND HAE JUNG ARE.

THAT WAS JUST AN ACT.

THAT'S ONE OF THE WAYS THEY LIKE TO PLAY.

THEY LIKE TO SET THE SCENE, THEN ACT IT OUT.

I LOVE YOU.
I LOVE YOU, TOO, JIMMY.

HA HA HA HA
HA HA HA HA!
HA HA HA HA HA
HA HA HA HA!

HA HA HA
HA HA HA!
HA HA HA
HA HA HA!
I KNOW HE'S THE BOSS'S SON AND ALL, BUT HE REALLY BUGS ME. THEY'RE ALWAYS ACTING CRAZY.

JIMMY'S DAD OWNS A CAFÉ. THEY'RE PROBABLY OVER THERE. IT'S NOT FAR FROM HERE.

WE PLANNED TO MEET UP THERE AND PARTY TODAY.

JIMMY'S DREAM IS TO BECOME A MOVIE DIRECTOR/ACTOR/SINGER. HE WAS IN SHOW BIZ WHEN HE LIVED IN HONG KONG.

THAT FIGURES--THAT LOOK AND THAT DIALOGUE...

GUEST

HE'S A HUGE FAN OF HONG KONG MOVIE EVERYTHING HE SAYS DOES COMES RIGHT OU HONG KONG MOVIES

HE DRESSES LIKE A PUNK ROCKER. HE LIKES PUNK MUSIC.
DARTS SPORT
IT'S AMAZING. HIS PUNK ROCK LOOK IS EVEN WEIRDER THAN MARILYN MANSON'S.

THEY ACT IT OUT, AND SOMETIMES THEY EVEN TAPE THEMSELVES WITH A VIDEO CAMERA. BUT I THINK TODAY WAS JUST IMPROV. YOU WERE JUST UNLUCKY AND GOT SUCKED INTO THEIR GAME.
THE MORE I THINK ABOUT IT, THE MORE I REALIZE THOSE TWO ARE JUST PLAIN NUTS.

I TOLD YOU BEFORE...
WHEN WAS THAT?

THOSE GUYS ARE DANGEROUS! DON'T GET INVOLVED WITH THEM!

FORGET ABOUT HAE JUNG. THOSE TWO WILL NEVER BREAK UP.

YOU'VE GOT NO RIGHT TO TELL ME WHAT TO DO OR WHAT NOT TO DO ABOUT THEM.
WELL, ANYWAY... THAT'S JUST MY OPINION.

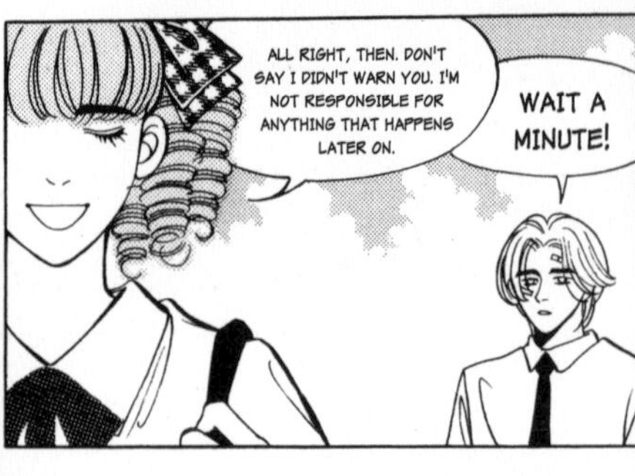

ALL RIGHT, THEN. DON'T SAY I DIDN'T WARN YOU. I'M NOT RESPONSIBLE FOR ANYTHING THAT HAPPENS LATER ON.
WAIT A MINUTE!

IF YOU WANT ME TO FORGET ABOUT HAE JUNG, WHY ARE YOU TAKING ME TO HER RIGHT NOW?

WELL, I HAVE TO ADMIT, IT'S PARTLY FOR MY OWN ENTERTAINMENT, BUT ALSO...

...I HATE JIMMY!

I WANT TO CAUSE A LITTLE TROUBLE BETWEEN THEM AND SEE IF THEY'LL BREAK UP. PLUS, I REALLY LIKE TO WATCH THEM FIGHT. IT'S SO COOL!

SOME BES
FRIEND...

WHAT ARE YOU DOING? ARE YOU CRAZY?! YOU'RE DRINKING STRAIGHT OUT OF THE BOTTLE!

MORON! YOU THOUGHT IT WAS REALLY LIQUOR?
IF THIS WERE REAL WHISKEY, I'D BE DEAD!

HMM? SHE'S RIGHT! IT'S JUST WATER!
I WAS JUST IMITATING A SCENE FROM *SWORDSMAN*.
IN THE MOVIE *SWORDSMAN*, THERE'S A SCENE WHERE CHUNG HA LIM POURS BOOZE STRAIGHT INTO HER MOUTH.
SWIG SWIG!
HONG KONG KARATE DUDE

BUT...

YOU BRAVELY STROLL RIGHT IN MY HIDEOUT?

GET THAT TOY GUN OUT OF MY FACE!

YOU THINK THIS IS A TOY? I DON'T LIKE FAKES. I ONLY LIKE THE REAL THING.

KNOW THIS. JIMMY ONLY LIKES THE REAL THING.

IF YOU UNDERSTAND, GET DOWN ON YOUR KNEES!

HOW DARE YOU LOOK DOWN AT M

IF THERE'S ANYTHING JIMMY HATES, IT'S PEOPLE WHO ARE TALLER THAN HIM!

EVEN I CAN'T WEAR HIGH HEELS AROUND JIMMY.

'CAUSE WHEN I WEAR HIGH HEELS, I'M TALLER THAN HIM.
하하하하
SHUT YOUR MOUTH!

HOW... HOW DID I GET MYSELF INTO THIS? HE HAD A REAL GUN...

I'M SCARED!

WHAT ARE YOU DOING HERE?

I BROUGHT HIM.

VOL. 5
Aspirin

SAY IT AGAIN.
YOU CAME
BECAUSE OF WHO?!

BECAUSE OF
HAE JUNG!

SAY IT AGAIN! YOU LITTLE BASTARD!

SAY IT AGAIN! YOU BASTARD!

BECAUSE OF HAE JUNG SHIN!

AGAIN!

BECAUSE I LIKE HAE JUNG

NO!

YOU'RE NOT EVEN FIT TO BE A DEMON!

YOU'RE JUST A CLOWN WHO WANTS TO BE COOL. YOU PSYCHO IDIOT!

YOU!

STOP IT!

JIMMY! STOP IT! YOU'LL KILL HIM!

HAE JUNG! STOP HIM! HOW CAN YOU JUST STAND THERE WHEN SUNG MOO'S ABOUT TO DIE FOR YOU?

HAE JUNG!

THAT'S RIGHT, HAE JUNG! THAT'S WHAT IT IS! YOUR PERFECT COLDNESS! YOUR TOTAL HEARTLESSNESS!
A PERSON CAN BE DY
RIGHT NEXT TO YOU AN
WOULDN'T EVEN BAT
EYELASH! YOU'RE SO C
SO SELFISH! I REAL
ADMIRE THAT!

K!
THAT'S WHY I LIKE YOU! I RESPECT YOU ! I LOVE YOU!
E JUNG! YOU'RE O COOL! YOU'RE STING YOURSELF N JIMMY! JUST AK UP WITH HIM!
H-HUH... I MUST BE GOING CRAZY!
JIMMY! DO WHATEVER YOU WANT; JUST DON'T BREAK ANYTHING! LAST TIME, I STEPPED ON A PIECE OF GLASS AND SLICED MY FOOT WIDE OPEN!
THAT'S YOUR JOB! YOU GET PAID TO BE HERE! YOU THINK IT'S EASY MONEY?!
T WASN'T FOR HAE JUNG, OULDN'T BE HERE, AMONG ESE LUNATICS! FOR THE FIRST TIME TODAY, I REALIZED THAT I AM TTERLY NORMAL... TOO RMAL. NO, I'M THANKFUL FOR MY NORMALCY. M, THANK YOU SO MUCH R GIVING BIRTH TO A NORMAL PERSON!
IF I CAN JUST GET OUT OF THIS HELLHOLE ALIVE, I PROMISE I'LL WASH THE BLEACH OUT OF MY HAIR. I'LL STOP DITCHING SCHOOL. I'LL COME HOME EARLY. I'LL EVEN LISTEN TO EVERYTHING YOU SAY, MOM!

THIS SUCKS!
IT SUCKS BECAUSE JIMMY IS THE ONLY ONE DOING THE HITTING. SUNG MOO'S JUST GETTING HIT! ISN'T THIS FIGHT A BIT TOO ONE-SIDED?
HEY! EVEN IN STREET FIGHTER VIRTUAL FIGHTER WOULD BE GAME O BY THIS TIME!
SO...
...DOES THAT MEAN THAT I CAN HIT JIMMY BACK?
OF COURSE!

THANKS!
YOU THINK I WASN'T FIGHTING BACK BECAUSE I DON'T KNOW HOW?
I WAS RESTRAINING MYSELF BECAUSE OF HAE JUNG! YOU LITTLE CAT-EYED FREAK!
I LOST MY CONTACT LENS...!

HAE JUNG! LET'S GO! LET'S GET OUTTA THIS FREAKHOUSE!
IF WE STAY HERE ANOTHER MINUTE, WE REALLY WILL GO CRAZY!

THAT WAS ABSOLUTELY AMAZING!

THAT'S IT! THAT'S SPIRIT!

AT'S RIGHT! FROM THE
ENT I SAW YOU, I COULD
THAT SPIRIT IN THOSE
OPY EYES UNDER THOSE
THICK EYEBROWS.
YOU SEE? I DID IT AGAIN! I DISCOVERED ANOTHER FUTURE STAR!
HEY, YOU! DID YOU GET ALL THAT ON FILM?!
THERE SEEMS TO HAVE BEEN A PERSON RESPONSIBLE FOR THE LIGHTING AND EVERYTHING.
YES SIR!
WHAT...
WHAT IS THIS?!
HEY, NOW! LET ME INTRODUCE YOU PROPERLY!

THIS IS SUNG MOO J
WHO IS MY MEAL
TICKET... ER... I MEAN,
NEWEST STAR AS O
TODAY!

SO, FROM HERE ON OUT, JUST HAVE FAITH IN ME AND DO WHAT I TELL YOU.
I'M GOING TO HONE AND REFINE THAT SPIRIT INSIDE YOU AND MAKE YOU INTO MY BIGGEST STAR YET!

BO NA!
I ONLY LIED A LITTLE BIT! I JUST DID WHAT JIMMY TOLD ME TO DO... I BROUGHT YOU HERE.

HAE JUNG!

WHAT DO YOU THINK?

ISN'T THIS FUN?

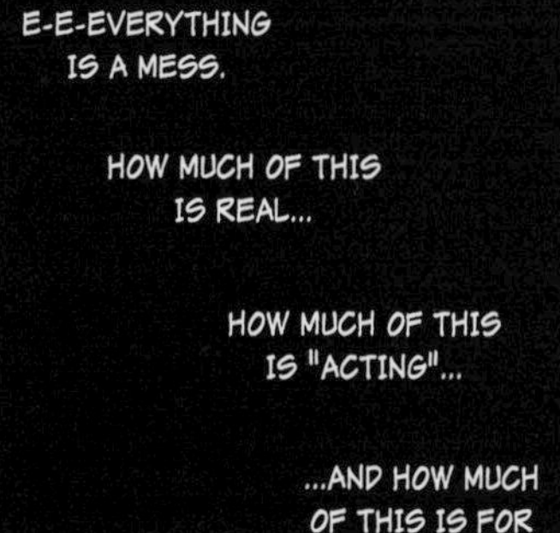

I'M "NORMAL."
I'M JUST A "TYPICAL," "ORDINARY" GUY!
SUNG MOO!
I JUST LIKE A GIRL AND WANT TO DO WHAT SHE WANTS ME TO DO.
AH, BUT THIS GIRL IS WAY TOO MUCH FOR ME!
IT'S BECOME UNBEARABLE, BABY. JUST THE THOUGHT OF BECOMING AN ADULT IS EXCRUCIATING TO ME.
HIS CUT OPENED UP! HE'S BLEEDING AGAIN!
JIMMY!
IS ALL
FAULT!
GOING
HE'S UNCONSCIOUS!
ooh! help me!

I LOVE YOU SO MUCH, MY LOVE. I LOVE YOU, BUT IT'S SO HARD TO MAKE UP MY MIND.
ENNH...

MAYBE YOU NEED A GUY WHO WILL MAKE YOU HAPPY WITH A NEW ADVENTURE EVERYDAY.
OH, MY LOVE... YOU TORTURE ME ALL THE TIME.
SOMETIMES, I THINK I NEED A BREAK FROM ALL OF THIS.

UNHH... H-H-HAE JUNG.

AH! YOU'VE COME TO! SUNG MOO.
Oh my Love

SORRY!
I DIDN'T THINK ALL
THIS WOULD BE SUCH
A SHOCK TO YOU.
BUT THE DAYS WHEN I'M ALONE... OOH, OOH...
I'M EVEN MORE AFRAID...

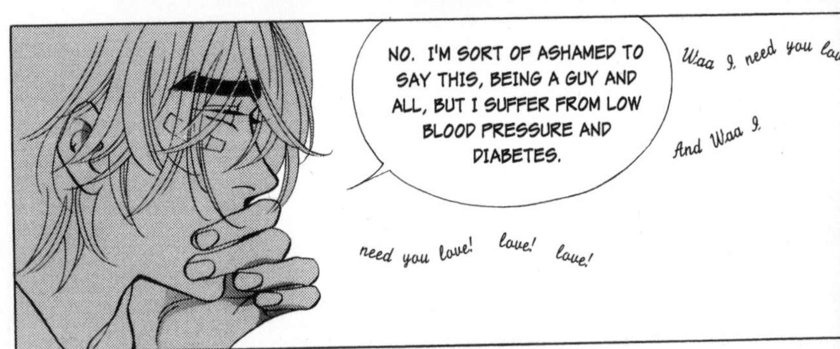
NO. I'M SORT OF ASHAMED TO SAY THIS, BEING A GUY AND ALL, BUT I SUFFER FROM LOW BLOOD PRESSURE AND DIABETES.
Waa I, need you love.
And Waa I,
need you love! love! love!

I'M SO AFRAID, BECAUSE
I KEEP FALLING DEEPER
INTO YOU. SHIT!
I'M SORRY.
I DIDN'T KNOW

I need you love!

And Waa I, need you love!

WHAT'S THIS SONG? IT'S THE FIRST TIME I'VE HEARD IT.

YEAH, IT'S CALLED "ASPIRIN," BY GIRL!

love!

love!

love!

IRIN... THAT'S T... THERE WAS MMERCIAL LIKE HAT WHEN I WAS A KID.

"IN THE MORNING, MY BROTHER AND I WERE HAVING A WATER FIGHT. LATER THAT NIGHT, BOTH OF US WERE VERY SICK."

"BUT, MY MOM GAVE ME TWO TABLETS OF ASPIRIN AND MY BROTHER FOUR TABLETS. WE WENT TO SLEEP AND THE NEXT DAY..."

THERE WAS A PARODY ON THIS COMMERCIAL.

"MOM GAVE US ASPIRIN AND I TOOK 20 TABLETS WHILE MY BROTHER TOOK 40."

"AND THE NEXT DAY...

...I WAS UNCONSCIOUS AND MY BROTHER WAS

HA HA HA HA HA!
SHIT! IT WAS J A JOKE! WHY THEY HAVE TO M SUCH AN AWF PARODY OUT OF WHAT KIND C PEOPLE WOUL THINK UP SOMETHING LI THAT? IT'S SIC

HEE HEE HEE! HA HA HA HA HA!
IT WAS PROBABLY SOMEONE LIKE JIMMY.
I'VE IT

E YOU LAUGHING
OURSELF LIKE
, LIKE A MONK
EEN STRUCK BY
NING? LIKE A
ZY PERSON?!
RE NOT HURT
NYMORE?!

A MONK STRUCK BY LIGHTNING?
WELL, Y'KNOW HOW THERE'S A SAYING THAT A MONK STANDING IN THE RAIN WILL MUMBLE TO HIMSELF? SO I FIGURE, A MONK WHO IS STRUCK BY LIGHTNING WILL LAUGH TO HIMSELF!

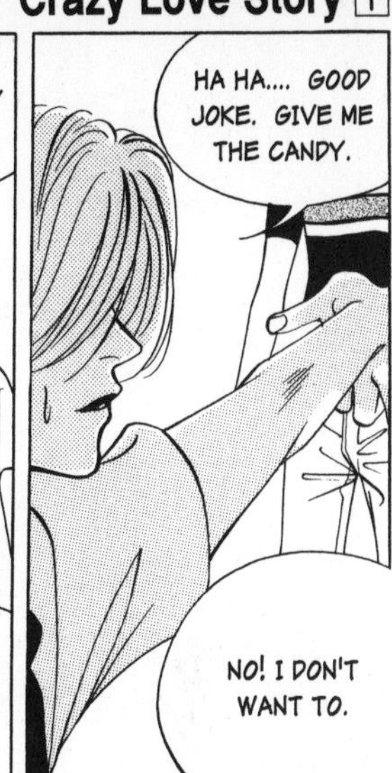
HA HA.... GOOD JOKE. GIVE ME THE CANDY.
NO! I DON'T WANT TO.

I'M GONNA EAT IT MYSELF!

AH...!

FINE. BUT I'LL GIVE IT TO YOU.

N-NO! THE LOW BLOOD-SUGAR LEVEL MAKES MY BREATH SMELL REALLY SWEET!
THAT'S OKAY!

THE CANDY'S... SWEET, TOO.
THAT PARODY ON ASPI
WAS TELLING US THA
TAKEN IN MODERATIO
ASPIRIN IS MEDICINE
BUT TOO MUCH OF A
GOOD THING CAN KILL

I HAD A BAD FEELING THAT THIS GIRL MIGHT STILL TURN OUT TO BE MY "ASPIRIN."
SHE'S MY MEDICINE... AND THE MEDICINE SHE GAVE ME WAS WORKING, TOO.
ARE YOU OKAY NOW?
Waa! I need you Love. And Waa, I need you love.
I'm scared of falling into you. Shit! Where will I find something like this again?

I'LL FORGIVE YOU FOR BORROWING MY FIANCÉE'S LIPS!

BECAUSE I'M THE ONE WHO MADE YOU SICK!

THAT'S VERY GENEROUS OF YOU, JIMMY. I'M REALLY TOUCHED.

SHIT! I GUESS THAT LINE WASN'T PART OF THE SCRIPT! FIANCÉE? CRAP!

JIMMY'S NOT AS CRAZY AS YOU THINK. HE'S VERY WARM-HEARTED, AND HE'S A REALLY GOOD GUY!

HE SEEMS A BIT PSYCHO, BUT ONLY BECAUSE HE'S A GENIUS! WE ALL NEED TO UNDERSTAND THAT.

HMMPH! IF ACTING LIKE A PSYCHO ON PURPOSE MAKES YOU A GENIUS, I'D BE A GENIUS TOO.

M SORRY MY ACTING WAS
ITTLE OVERBOARD TODAY.
OU GOT
JRT ON
CCOUNT
OF ME.
AS LONG AS
YOU'RE THE ONE
DOING THE
HITTING, I'M OKAY
WITH IT...

EVEN IF I GET KICKED
DOWN THE STAIRS.

MOM!

THIS IS FAR
IOUGH! I'LL GO ON
OWN FROM HERE.
IE FOLLOWED
ME AGAIN!
VEN TODAY...

MY MOM IS
WAITING
FOR ME!

WHENEVER I'M OUT LATE,
MY MOM FOLLOWS ME
UNTIL I GET HOME.

THAT'S ENOUGH! I'M HERE!

THIS IS AS FAR AS YOU GO! YOU KNOW YOU CAN'T COME IN THE HOUSE, RIGHT?

IN THE HOUSE ARE MY OLDER SISTER, MY YOUNGER SISTER, DAD, AND THAT WOMAN-- OUR "FAMILY"!

AND HOME...!

VOL. 6 S·H·E

IS THAT YOU, HAE JUNG?

YEAH.

DID YOU JUST COME FROM THE LIBRARY?
YEAH.

POP!
I DIDN'T HEAR THE CAR JUST NOW. DIDN'T YOU TAKE THE LIBRARY CAR?
I WALKED.

DO YOU STILL THINK ABOUT MOM?

WHAT ARE YOU TALKING ABOUT?

IT WAS A LITTLE WHILE AFTER MOM PASSED AWAY, WHEN YOU WERE IN NINTH GRADE, I THINK...
YOU RAN HOME CRYING, SAYING THAT MOM WAS FOLLOWING YOU... ISN'T THAT WHAT HAPPENED?

I DON'T REMEMBER.

YOU'VE CHANGED SINCE THEN.

YOU HAVEN'T CHANGED ON THE OUTSIDE, BUT INSIDE, SOMETHING'S DIFFERENT.

DO YOU STILL SEE MOM SOMETIMES?
HOW CAN I SEE HER?

SHE'S DEAD.

WHY AREN'T YOU WEARING YOUR GLASSES? YOU HAVE BAD EYES.

I DON'T WANT TO SEE THIS WORLD.

ISN'T IT UNCOMFORTABLE?
PREMIUM
ORANGE JUCE
100
I'M USED TO IT.

YOU KNOW WHAT? WHEN PEOPLE'S EYES OR EARS DON'T WORK LIKE THEY SHOULD, THEIR OTHER SENSES BECOME MORE DEVELOPED, TO COMPENSATE.
THEY START TO SEE AND HEAR WITH THOSE OTHER SENSES.
THERE'S A C OVER THER RIGHT?

ONLY, I CAN'T SEE THE CUP.
BECAUSE I'M NEARSIG I CAN'T SEE ANYTHING THAN A FOOT AWA ANYTHING FARTHER THAT BECOMES HA AND UNCLEAR.

STILL, I KNOW THERE'S A CUP OVER THERE.

BECAUSE EVEN THOUGH I CAN'T SEE THE CUP, I CAN **FEEL** THAT THE CUP IS THERE.

I KNOW THE CUP IS THERE, BUT NOT BY HABIT.

Y VISION IS SO BAD THAT MY EYES CAN'T DELIVER HE MESSAGE TO MY BRAIN THAT THERE'S A CUP OVER THERE.

I JUST FEEL THE CUP THERE.

SOMETIMES, YOU'RE SO STUBBORN. YOU'VE BEEN THAT WAY SINCE YOU WERE LITTLE.
ME?
DON'T YOU REMEMBER?
ONE TIME MOM FOUND YOU ON THE FRONT LAWN DIGGING UP DIRT AND EATING IT.

SURE, A LOT OF KIDS TRY EATING PAPER OR DIRT, BUT MOM DIDN'T WANT THAT TO BECOME A HABIT FOR YOU, SO YOU GOT INTO A LOT OF TROUBLE.

SHE WAS SURE YOU'D NEVER DO IT AGAIN, BECAUSE YOU CRIED YOUR EYES OUT WHEN SHE PUNISHED YOU.
THEN ONE DAY, YOU BROUGHT A HANDFUL OF DIRT INTO THE HOUSE...
...AND RIGHT IN FRONT OF
YOU STARTED EATING
LIKE YOU WANTED HER TO SEE YOU

DO YOU REMEMBER THAT?
NOPE.

IT'S LATE. GO UPSTAIRS AND GO TO SLEEP.
I WILL. YOU NEED TO EAT, THOUGH.

FIND SOMETHING EAT. BUT FIRST, I'M GONNA GO WASH UP.
YEAH, OKAY.

OF COURSE I REMEMBER. I DID THAT ON PURPOSE.

I'VE BEEN THAT WAY SINCE I WAS LITTLE. WHENEVER MY MOM TOLD ME NOT TO DO THIS, NOT TO DO THAT...
...I WOULD STAND RIGHT IN FRONT OF HER ON PURPOSE AND DO EXACTLY WHAT SHE JUST TOLD ME NOT TO DO.

THAT'S PROBABLY THE PSYCHOLOGY OF CHILDREN DOING SOMETHING JUST BECAUSE WE'RE TOLD NOT TO.
ESPECIALLY WITH PEOPLE WE LOVE, WITH PEOPLE WE WANT ATTENTION FROM.
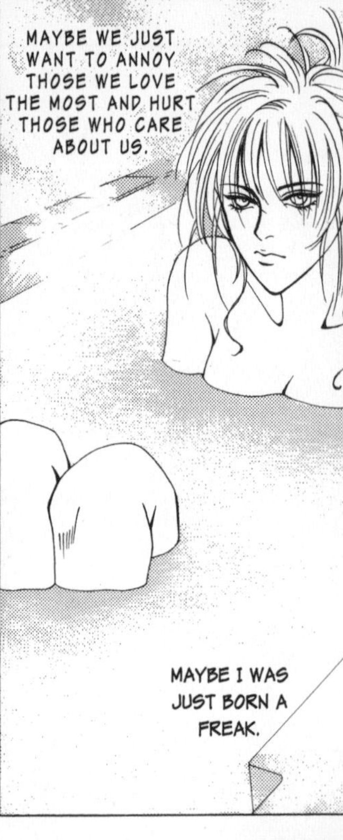
MAYBE WE JUST WANT TO ANNOY THOSE WE LOVE THE MOST AND HURT THOSE WHO CARE ABOUT US.
MAYBE I WAS JUST BORN A FREAK.

KNOCK! KNOCK!
OH! ARE YOU HOME, HAE JUNG?

WERE YOU STUDYING LATE?

ISN'T STUDYING HARD?
AREN'T YOU HUNGRY?

I ALREADY ATE WITH MY FRIENDS.
YOU GO AHEAD AND GO TO BED. I'M JUST GOING TO WASH UP, AND THEN I'M GOING TO SLEEP, TOO.

IT'S GOOD THAT OU'RE STUDYING, JT DON'T STAY OUT TOO LATE...

OF COURSE, YOU'RE O SMART THAT YOUR AD AND I DON'T HAVE O WORRY TOO MUCH ABOUT YOU.
MY DAD BROUGHT THIS WOMAN INTO THE HOUSE LESS THAN A YEAR AFTER MY MOM DIED.

WE ALREADY KNEW HER. WHEN I WAS VERY YOUNG, MY DAD'S BUSINESS WENT BANKRUPT. HE HAD TO GO INTO HIDING, AND SHE WAS THE WOMAN WHO HID HIM.

I KNOW THAT MUCH. AT LEAST, IT'S WHAT I'VE HEARD.

I'M TELLING YOU AGAIN--I DON'T WANT YOU OUT TOO LATE.
DON'T TELL ME WHAT TO DO!

THE ONLY PERSON IN THIS WORLD WHO HAS THE RIGHT TO TELL ME WHAT TO DO IS MY MOM.

GO TO SLEEP.

FINE.

THAT'S MY MOM'S ROOM!

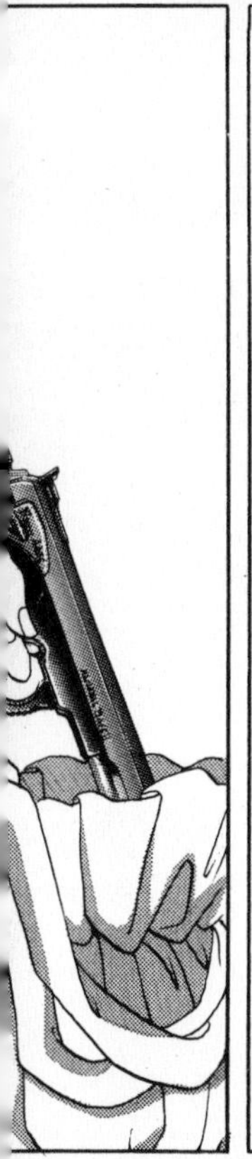

ONCE, SUNG MOO ASKED ME IF I STOLE THINGS BECAUSE I WAS ON MY PERIOD. THAT'S DEFINITELY NOT WHY.

AND BECAUSE STEALING I
WRONG, I ONLY DO IT IF A RE
STRONG URGE COMES OVER

THAT'S RIGHT. EVERY TIME I SEE MY MOM'S GHOST, I HAVE TO STEAL. THAT'S THE ONLY THING THAT MAKES ME FEEL CALM. IT'S KINDA LIKE WHEN I USED TO DO ALL SORTS OF BAD THINGS IN FRONT OF HER WHEN I WAS LITTLE.

WHAT AM I GONNA DO? MY WALLET'S GONE!
DID YOU LOOK CAREFULLY? MAYBE YOU LEFT IT AT HOME, OR MAYBE YOU DROPPED IT SOMEWHERE?
AFTER I WENT TO THE STUDENT STORE AN HOUR AGO, I PUT IT IN MY BAG!
COURSE, AT FIRST, MY "SINS" 'T JUST CONSIST OF STEALING.
I KNOW I LEFT IT HERE!
PEOPLE FEEL SO FRUSTRATED AND CONFUSED WHEN THEY LOSE SOMETHING.
I TRIED LOTS OF THINGS, BUT AS I REMEMBER, THAT WOMAN'S REACTION WHEN I STOLE HER DIAMOND RING GAVE ME REAL SATISFACTION.
H NO! MY RING IS ISSING!!
CALDER
calde
gaferie
KU
AND AS I WATCHED THIS, I FELT JOY.

OF COURSE,
EVERYTHING I STEAL,
I ALWAYS THROW AWAY.

IF YOU KEEP WHAT YOU STEAL, THEN STEALING LOSES ITS MEANING.
THE ACT IS COMPLETE ONLY WHEN YOU THROW THE STOLEN GOODS AWAY.

AH, I FEEL TOTAL PEACE AND HAPPINESS.

IF IT WAS AN HOUR AGO, THEN WE WERE IN P.E. CLASS. WHO WAS IN THE ROOM THEN?
JU BUN...

MAYBE!

LEAVE IT!
/E STOLE IT JUST
O THROW IT AWAY
ANYHOW!

LOOK THROUGH
HE TRASH CAN!
'S PROBABLY IN
THERE!

YOU'RE RIGHT! WHOEVER STOLE IT MAY HAVE JUST TAKEN THE MONEY AND THROWN THE WALLET IN THE TRASH!

HERE IT IS...
... AS EXPECTED.
THAT'S WEIRD! THE MONEY'S STILL IN IT!

THAT REALLY IS STRANGE.
WHO WOULD HAVE DONE...

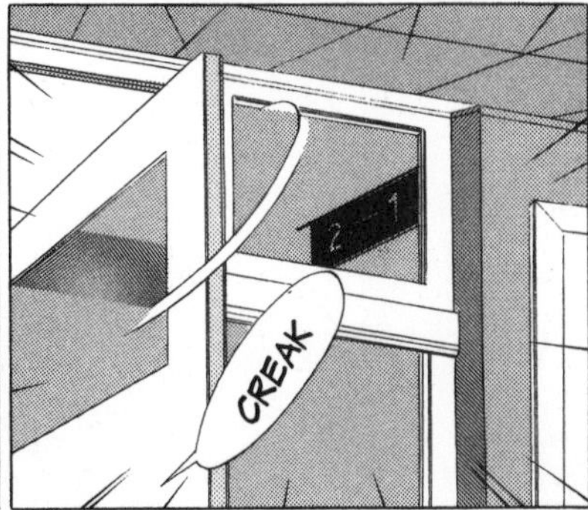
CREAK

WHAT'S WRONG?
DID SOMETHING HAPPEN?

I NEED TO TALK TO YOU FOR A MINUTE, HAE JUNG.

WHAT?

YOU DID IT, DIDN'T YOU?!

YOU STOLE THAT GIRL'S WALLET AND THREW IT AWAY!

OW DO YOU KNOW...
...IF IT WAS ME OR NOT?

HAE JUNG.
I REALLY LIKE YOU A LOT, BUT I DON'T THINK I KNOW YOU.
WHICH SIDE OF YOU IS THE REAL YOU?
YOU MET ME AT THE ROCK CAFÉ AND MADE ME STEAL A CAR...
.AND YOU KISSED ME FIRST, BUT ALL OF A SUDDEN, YOU CT COLD TOWARDS ME, KICK ME DOWN A FLIGHT OF STAIRS, MAKE ME ROLL ALL THE WAY DOWN...
THEN YOU PLAN IT WITH JIMMY TO MAKE ME LOOK LIKE A FOOL, AND TELL ME THAT IT WAS ALL AN "ACT" AND ALL FOR "PLAY"...
AND THEN, AFTER THAT, YOU ACT NICE TO ME AGAIN.

WHAT AM
TO YOU?

WHEN I FEEL LIKE THINGS ARE GETTING COMPLICATED, OR WHEN I'M NERVOUS, I NEED TO STEAL SOMETHING SO I CAN FEEL CALM AGAIN.

LIKING JIMMY IS THE SAME THING.

WHEN I'M WITH HIM, WITH BOTH OF US ACTING CRAZY AND CAUSING TROUBLE, I FEEL CALM.

LISTEN! I'LL BE HONEST WITH YOU!

I'VE BEEN PLAYING WITH YOU ALL THIS TIME! DON'T YOU GET IT?! YOU IDIOT!

THEN, EVERYTHING THAT HAPPENED IN JIMMY'S CAFÉ?!
FROM BEGINNING TO END, I PLAYED WITH YOU! WE PLAYE WITH YOU--JIMMY AND I! EVEN NA WAS IN ON THE PLAN! DO YO REALLY THINK THAT I COULD HA KISSED YOU IN FRONT OF JIMMY THAT HE WOULD LET ME DO THAT IF THAT WAS FOR REAL, JIMMY WOULD HAVE KILLED ME!

YOU SAID THAT WAS ALL PART OF THE ACT. YOU SAID IT WAS ALL FOR THE SAKE OF JIMMY'S MOVIE.
WHAT THE HELL ARE YOU TALKING ABOUT? WHAT MOVIE?! LIKE YOU SAID, THAT GUY'S JUST A DREAMER! HE'S SO CRAZY ABOUT ACTION FILMS THAT HE IMITATES THEM ALL THE TIME!
FROM THE BEGINNING! FROM THE BEGINNING TO THE END!
WE PLANNED ALL AND MADE A FOOL OUT OF YOU!

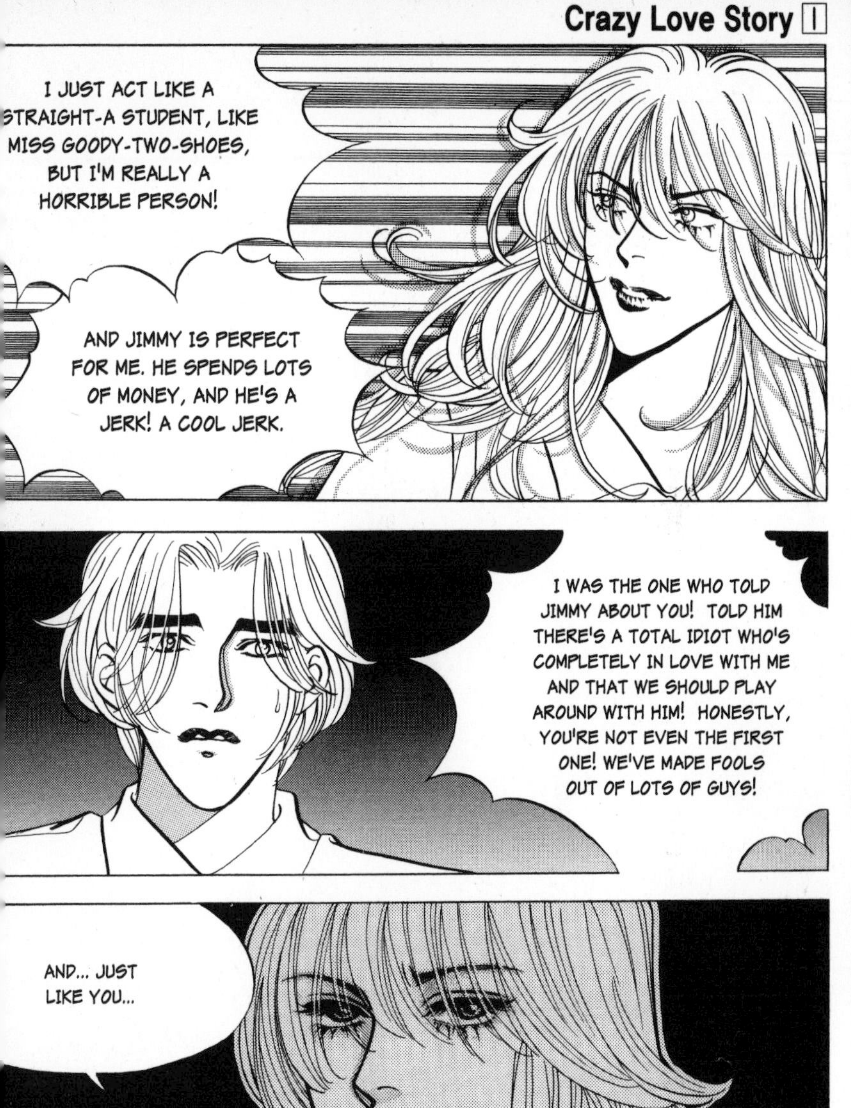
I JUST ACT LIKE A STRAIGHT-A STUDENT, LIKE MISS GOODY-TWO-SHOES, BUT I'M REALLY A HORRIBLE PERSON!
AND JIMMY IS PERFECT FOR ME. HE SPENDS LOTS OF MONEY, AND HE'S A JERK! A COOL JERK.
I WAS THE ONE WHO TOLD JIMMY ABOUT YOU! TOLD HIM THERE'S A TOTAL IDIOT WHO'S COMPLETELY IN LOVE WITH ME AND THAT WE SHOULD PLAY AROUND WITH HIM! HONESTLY, YOU'RE NOT EVEN THE FIRST ONE! WE'VE MADE FOOLS OUT OF LOTS OF GUYS!
AND... JUST LIKE YOU...
...I PICKED UP THOSE MORONS... IN A ROCK CAFÉ OR SOMEWHERE LIKE IT, JUST LIKE I DID WITH YOU.

VOL. 7
Your cruel heart

I-I'M...
...CONFUSED ENOUGH AS IT IS, JUST WITH MYSELF.

......
I-I NEVER TOLD YOU, BUT I'VE LIKED YOU SINCE BEFORE YOU EVEN KNEW ME.
......

YOU SHOULDN'T LIKE GIRLS FOR THE WRONG REASONS, LIKE BECAUSE THEY HAVE A NICE BODY, OR LONG HAIR, OR A PRETTY FACE OR PRETTY LEGS.

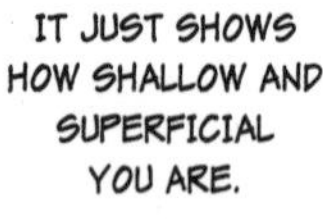
IT JUST SHOWS HOW SHALLOW AND SUPERFICIAL YOU ARE.

THAT'S NOT IT. I DON'T LIKE YOU FOR THOSE REASONS.

IT WAS FUN WHILE IT LASTED. TOYING WITH YOU, THAT IS.
BUT NOW, I'M BORED OF IT.

GOODBYE.
STAY AWAY FROM ME.
OU'RE NOT THE
AME TYPE OF
ERSON AS US.
I CAN TELL BY YOUR EYES.

I SAID IT'S OVER! YOU IDIOT!

IT WAS ALREADY MAY, BUT THAT POOL WAS TOO COLD FOR MY HEART.
HER COLD WORDS AND COLD FACE FROZE MY HEART EVEN MORE.

FROM UNDERWATER, I COULD SEE THE MAY SKY AND THE MAY BREEZE THAT WERE STILL TOO COLD FOR SPRING.
FROM UNDERWATER, THAT MAY SKY LOOKED SO COLD.
MY HEART WAS BURNING WITH THE FEVER OF LOVE, BEATING WITH YOUTH.
MY LOVE...
...WAS DROWNING...
...IN THAT BLUE MAY WATER.

DON'T BE ATTRACTED BY ME.

THE WORLD I'M LIVING IN IS MORE FRIGHTENING THAN YOU THINK.

WE LIVE IN TOTALLY DIFFERENT WORLDS.

EVENTUALLY, I KILL EVERYONE IN MY WORLD.

DON'T TRY AND COME INTO MY WORLD. JUST STAY THERE IN THE WATER. DON'T EVEN TRY TO GET OUT. YOU'LL BE SORRY. I'M NOT WORTH IT.

I'M ACTUALLY DOING YOU A FAVOR. YOU SHOULD BE THANKFUL, STUPID. SO JUST GO.

HAE JUNG!

HAE JUNG.

HAE
JUNG...

YOU CAN CLOSE
ME OUT OF
YOUR HEART.
BUT WITH
ALL MY HEART,
I LOVE YOU.
BOMB... THIS GUY
IS THE BOMB...

I LOVE
YOU...

AH!
번쩍
WHAT... WHAT ARE YOU DOING?!
휘익
ACK!
풍덩
WHA...
WHAT THE HELL ARE YOU DOING?
SORRY. THE WATER'S COLD, HUH?
...

THIS IS ONLY THE BEGINNING.

I'M NOT GOING TO GIVE UP!

EVEN IF I HAD NO TAIL TO SWIM WITH AND NO TONGUE TO SING WITH. I WANTED TO WALK...

OUR LOVE WAS STILL MELTING IN A COLD MAY POOL.

...WALK IN HAE JUNG'S WORLD.

FINE! DO WHAT YOU WANT! YOU STUBBORN BASTARD!
DO WHAT YOU WANT WITH YOUR HEART OR WITH... WHATEVER!
ACHOO!
SORRY.

JUST REMEMBER--
I'M NEVER GOING TO LIKE YOU BACK.

WE'LL SEE.

WANNA BET?

YOU MAKE ME SICK! YOU'RE EVEN MORE PSYCHO THAN JIMMY!

HAE JUNG!

YOU BOTH LEFT SO SUDDENLY, AND YOU DIDN'T COME BACK AFTER LUNCHTIME.
WHAT HAPPENED? DID YOU GUYS GO SWIMMING OR SOMETHING?

THAT BASTARD THREW ME IN THE WATER.
LET'S SEE... A HANDKER-CHIEF...

H-H-HERE!

TAKE IT!

......
......
......

W-WAIT! I'LL SQUEEZE IT OUT FOR YOU...!
IT'S FINE!

ISN'T THAT THE SAME HANDKERCHIEF I SAT ON LAST TIME?

DIDN'T YOU EVEN WASH IT?
......

B-BUT A GIRL WHO DOESN'T CARRY A HANDKERCHIEF IS EVEN WORSE.

NOTHING'S MORE UNAPPEALING THAN A GUY WHO CARRIES A HANDKERCHIEF.

I'VE GOT ONE, STUPID.

STARTING NOW...

...IT'S SUMMER.

HOW MANY SUMMERS HAVE TO PASS BEFORE I WIN YOUR HEART?

WOW! LOOK HOW TALL HE IS!

MY GOODNESS! KIDS THESE DAYS ARE SO BIG! IF ONLY MY SON YOON GI WAS THAT TALL.

CRAZY KIDS! I CAN'T BELIEVE THEIR PARENTS LET THEM GET AWAY WITH THAT!

OBVIOUSLY, THEY HAVE BAD PARENTS. THAT'S WHY THEY'RE LIKE THAT.

MOM!

I TOLD YOU. WHEN WE'RE ON THE STREET, JUST PRETEND YOU DON'T KNOW ME.
CRUNCH
BUT THIS IS OUR HOME.

JUST NOW, I WAS COMING IN WITH YOON GI'S MOM AND JANG HUN'S MOM AND DO YOU KNOW WHAT THEY SAID ABOUT YOU?
I HEARD EVERY WORD. HEH HEH...

THEY JUST COULDN'T RECOGNIZE YOU BECAUSE YOU GOT SO TALL ALL OF SUDDEN, BUT IF THEY HAD RECOGNIZED YOU.
...YOU'D BE THE LAUGHINGSTOCK OF THE NEIGHBORHOOD. HEH HEH HEH...

IF YOU KNOW THAT...
...GET IN THERE AND WASH THAT YELLOW OUT OF YOUR HAIR!

IF YOU GIVE ME MONEY, I'LL GO AND DO IT.
WHAT HAPPENED TO THE MONEY I GAVE YOU LAST TIME?!

WHERE ARE YOU GOING? GET BACK HERE RIGHT NOW!
I NEED TO CHANGE AND GO OUT.
I BOUGHT CLOTHES.
WHY, YOU LITTLE...!!!
MY PART-TIME JOB!
NOW WHERE ARE YOU GOING?!
HMPH... YOU CALL THAT MONEY?!
HAVEN'T I GIVEN YOU ENOUGH MONEY? WHAT DO YOU MEAN, PART-TIME JOB?!

TAKE IT.

THIS IS MY FRIEND'S UNCLE'S STORE. AFTER SCHOOL, I COME HERE TO WORK PART-TIME.

HEY! YOU'RE HERE!

HI!

BECAUSE MY MOM'S SO STINGY, I ALWAYS NEED TO WORK PART-TIME. I NEED TO BUY CLOTHES, CDS, HAVE FUN—AND WHEN YOU GO OUT TO PARTY, YOU NEED MONEY. IN THIS WORLD, YOU CAN'T DO ANYTHING WITHOUT MONEY.

EH? YOU COME TO WORK WEARING SUNGLASSES?

C'MON! THERE ARE HARDLY ANY CUSTOMERS. SINCE NO ONE'S HERE, LET'S DANCE. LET'S PARTY!

YEAH, WE WERE JUST SAYING THE SAME THING.

THE OWNER'S NEPHEW

WE CALL IT A PART-TIME JOB, BUT THERE AREN'T MANY CUSTOMERS HERE. SO, AS YOU CAN SEE, WE DANCE HERE, SHOOT POOL HERE, AND PARTY LIKE IT'S OUR LITTLE HIDEOUT.

X-LARGE STORE

Let Die!

THE OWNER, MY FRIEND'S UNCLE, IS ALWAYS NAPPING.

WAIT A MINUTE!

LOOK AT THEM!

WE ALL MET AT A ROCK CAFE.
WHEN IT COMES TO DANCING,
E'VE NEVER LOST A COMPETITION.
WHEN WE STEP ON THE FLOOR,
VERYONE GETS OUT OF OUR WAY.
WE LOVE THAT, OF COURSE.

VOL. 8
The other country

FOR ME...

IT'S THAT TALL ONE IN THE MIDDLE!

THEY'RE TOO SKINNY, DON'T YOU THINK?
HE CAN'T EVEN CONTROL HIS OWN BODY.
HE DANCES LIKE A FREAK.
X-LARGE
NO.
HE MAY NOT HAVE MUCH TECHNIQUE...
...BUT HE GOT RHYT
EVEN HIS FINGERS ARE DANCING!
THAT GUY LOVES DANC
X-LARGE
HEY! WHERE ARE YOU GOING?
TO HIT ON HIM.

EXCUSE ME.
HOW'VE YOU BEEN?
WHO ARE YOU? DO I KNOW YOU?
SURE. WE JUST MET, RIGHT NOW.
THERE'S SOMETHING I WANT TO GIVE YOU.
WHAT'S THAT?
HERE!
DRINK THIS.
Budw
KING OF

HUH?
WHY? WHY ARE YOU GIVING ME THIS?
AREN'T YOU THIRSTY? DRINK IT.
UH...I'M UNDERAGE.

HA HA HA HA HA!
HA HA HA HA HA!
THAT'S HILARIOUS! HE'S A LITTLE HIGH SCHOOLER!
SO YUNG! WERE
THINKING

DUMBASS! YOU'RE NOT SUPPOSED TO SAY THAT!
UH... B-BUT!
MINORS WHO COME TO PLACES LIKE THIS AREN'T MINORS.
JUST TAKE IT. PRETEND IT'S YOUR BIG SISTER GIVING IT TO YOU.
SO YUNG! ARE INTO YOUNGER MEN? HA HA HA HA!
KNOCK IT OFF! IT'S SO EMBARRASSING!
SHUT UP!

PLEASE DRINK IT, MR. MINOR.
I'M BEGGING YOU.

BUT I'M NOT ALLOWED TO DRINK.

HEY! JUST DRINK IT FOR HER! DRINK IT!
SHE'S SO PRETTY! YOU'LL TOTALLY BUM HER OUT!
X-LARGE

I DON'T KNOW IF I SHOULD.
eiser®
BEERS
라이저

꿀꺽
OH WELL. WHAT THE HELL!
꿀꺽

HE DRANK IT! HE DRANK IT!
NOW YOU'RE IN TROUBLE. YOU'VE BEEN CAUGHT BY A WITCH.
ANYONE WHO DRINKS THE BEER SHE GIVES HIM FALLS UNDER HER SPELL.

HEY! MR. MINOR AND FRIENDS! WANT TO PARTY WITH US? WE'LL BUY THE DRINKS!

REALLY?!
WOW!

UM... WE DIDN' COME HERE TO PARTY.
WE WORK HERE. EVEN THOUGH WE DANCE AND HANG OUT WHEN THERE AREN'T TOO MANY CUSTOMERS, WHEN MORE START TO COME, WE HAVE TO HELP WITH THE SERVING...

SIR!
YES!
HE WAS NAPPING.

LOCK THE DOORS!
I'M TAKING THIS PLACE OVER FOR THE NIGHT.

M-MISS... THAT'S IMPOSSIBLE. TODAY'S SATURDAY, AND IT'S ONLY 5 PM...

HOW MUCH DO YOU WANT FOR IT?

I SAID, HOW MUCH?!

SIR! YOU BETTER TAKE HER SERIOUSLY.
잘 잘 잘
HER DAD'S A MILLIONAIRE! SHE COULD BUY THIS WHOLE CAFÉ IF SHE WANTED!

HEY! PUT UP THE "CLOSED" SIGN! AND LOCK THE DOORS!
YES, SIR!
-THIS IS MY LUCKY DAY!

EXCUSE ME!
MISS! WE'RE
CLOSED TODAY!

WE'RE
CLOSED
TODAY!

HEY,
LISTEN!

MISS... WE'RE NOT OPEN FOR BUSINESS TODAY...
WHAT'S THAT TALL CHICK'S PROBLEM?

KLAK!

MISS!

LOOK HERE, MISS!

TAK! TAK!

THEN WHO ARE THEY? AREN'T THEY CUSTOMERS?

AH! THAT'S NOT IT, MISS. TODAY, WE'RE HAVING A PRIVATE PARTY.
DON'T LIE!
I'M MEETING SOMEONE HERE AT 7 O'CLOCK.
YOU'RE CLOSING FOR NO REASON! ARE YOU TRYING TO RUIN MY IMPORTANT MEETING?

I'M RENTING THIS PLACE OUT FOR TODAY! SO PLEASE LEAVE THE PREMISES.

SIR! HOW MUCH IS SHE PAYING YOU?
HUH?
I SAID, HOW MUCH IS SHE PAYING TO RENT THIS PLACE OUT?
UH, THAT.

Crazy Love Story 1 END

재롱이 이야기
JERONGEE'S STORY
Zzz...
JERONGEE, THE CAT WHO SOMETIMES MAKES A SPECIAL APPEARANCE IN C.L.S., IS DOING VERY WELL.

AT 7 YEARS OLD, JERONGEE HAS REACHED RETIREMENT AGE. BUT HE STILL KEEPS HIMSELF BUSY.

YEEEEK!

HE'LL OFTEN GO OUT AND COME BAC
WITH A MOUSE OR A SPARROW
ONCE, HE EVEN BROUGHT BAC
A CHICK FROM SOMEWHERE

HERE'S A PRESENT, MEOW.

HIS TASTES ARE SIMPLE, BUT SOPHISTICATED.
HE ONLY EATS NAME-BRAND FOOD.
ARTIFICIAL CRABMEAT. HE EATS 3-4 PER DAY.

EVEN THOUGHT HE'S
CAT, JERONGEE WON
EVEN TOUCH FISH
OR MILK!
JERONGEE, I ROASTED YOU SOME FISH. TRY IT...
I JUST WANT M
NAME-BRAND FO
AND MY ARTIFIC
CRABMEAT!

BUT ONE DAY...
HUH? ISN'T THAT JERONGEE?
HE'S... DIGGING THROUGH THE TRASH!
DON'T I GIVE YOU A GOOD HOME AND GOOD FOOD?! HUH?!
THEN WHY ARE YOU DIGGING THROUGH THE TRASH LIKE A HOMELESS CAT?
OUCH!
캬웅
YOU LITTLE...!
HOW DARE YOU SCRATCH YOUR MOMMY? HUH? WHERE DID YOU LEARN TO DO THAT?! YOU LITTLE...!
캬악
W-WAIT, MS. LEE!
HE... HE DOESN'T LOOK LIKE JERONGEE. HIS FACE IS A LITTLE DIFFERENT.
HIS EYE COLOR WAS THE ONLY THING THAT DISTINGUISHED HIM FROM JERONGEE.
THIS POOR CAT HAD FINALLY FOUND SOMETHING TO EAT, BUT HE WAS CARRIED OFF BY A STRANGE WOMAN AND BEATEN HALF TO DEATH.
S-SORRY...
YOU SHOULD LOOK MORE CAREFULLY NEXT TIME!
MOMMY, WHAT HAPPENED?
I STILL SEE THAT CAT SOMETIMES, BUT I DON'T THINK HE'S FORGOTTEN ME YET.
HEY! JERONGEE'S TWIN! HOW'RE YOU DOING?
캬악
NONE OF YOUR BUSINESS!

In the next volume of

Sung Moo is a lone wolf who doesn't seem to care about anybody, but he's on the hunt for love and someone to care for him. On the other hand, all Jimmy cares about is money. He runs a division of his father's mafia business and extorts funds to produce movies. Stuck in the middle is Hae Jung, Jimmy's girlfriend, who is always being left alone with Sung Moo. This all spells a delicious--and dangerous--love triangle!

forbidden Dance™
by Hinako Ashihara

TOKYOPOP®
Dancing was her life...
Her dance partner
might be her future...
Available Now

T
TEEN
AGE 13+